UNLOCKING POTENTIAL

Insights, Tips & Strategies for Young Black People

Workbook

Anthony W. Scott, Esq.

Copyright © 2025 Anthony W. Scott, Esq.

All rights reserved.

No part of this publication may be reproduced, distributed, or transmitted in any form or by any means, including photocopying, recording, or other electronic or mechanical methods, without the prior written permission of the author, except in the case of brief quotations embodied in critical reviews and certain other non-commercial uses permitted by copyright law. For permission requests, please contact the publisher at the address below.

Published by:

I.S.I. Publishing, LLC

ISBN (e-book): 979-8-9920157-2-0

ISBN (print copy): 979-8-9920157-3-7

First Edition: March 1, 2025

This book is a work of nonfiction. While every effort has been made to ensure its accuracy, the author and publisher make no representations or warranties concerning the completeness or accuracy of the contents. The author and publisher disclaim any liability connected with the use of this information.

Designed and Printed in the United States of America

For additional resources or inquiries, contact:

I.S.I. Consulting, LLC

P.O. Box 29037, Parma, OH 44129,

info@isiconsultingllc.com

www.isiconsultingllc.com

Contents

Introduction 1

Chapter 1: Adaptability 6

Chapter 2: Appearance 13

Chapter 3: Authenticity 18

Chapter 4: Branding 23

Chapter 5: Career 29

Chapter 6: Character 36

Chapter 7: Communication 44

Chapter 8: Diversity, Equity, and Inclusion (DEI) 51

Chapter 9: Education 55

Chapter 10: Emotional Intelligence 60

Chapter 11: Entrepreneurship 68

Chapter 12: Finance 75

Chapter 13: Goal Setting 81

Chapter 14: Health and Wellness 86

Chapter 15: Management and Leadership 92

Chapter 16: Mentors and Sponsors 100

Chapter 17: Military 105

Chapter 18: Networking 108

Chapter 19: Mindset 114

Chapter 20: Professionalism 124

Chapter 21: Purpose & Passion 132

Chapter 22: Relationships 141

Chapter 23: Technology 148

Chapter 24: Volunteerism 154

Conclusion 159

Introduction

Welcome to the Unlocking Potential Workbook, designed to help you reflect, set goals, and create actionable steps toward personal and professional growth. This workbook offers a structured yet flexible approach to self-discovery, enabling you to bridge the gap between where you are and where you aspire to be.

Why This Workbook Matters

Success isn't linear; it's a journey filled with challenges and growth opportunities. This workbook acts as your:

- ☞ **Mirror:** Highlighting your skills, values, and areas for growth.
- ☞ **Map:** Guiding you in making purposeful career and life decisions.
- ☞ **Toolbox:** Offering exercises and strategies for achieving your potential.

This workbook turns theory into action, helping you navigate obstacles and stay aligned with your personal goals and values.

Who This Workbook Is For

This workbook is for anyone ready to take charge of their journey—students, professionals, career shifters, and those navigating systemic barriers. It provides guidance for balancing authenticity with professionalism, building confidence, and tackling high-stakes situations.

What You'll Gain

By the end of this workbook, you'll have:

Clarity on Goals and Values: Understand what matters most and align your life accordingly.

- **Practical Tools:** Strategies for networking, resilience, and professional success.
- **Authentic Confidence:** Learn to embrace your identity while meeting career expectations.
- **Resilience Skills:** Adapt to change and bounce back from setbacks optimistically.
- **A Growth Plan:** Create actionable, measurable steps for continued development.

How to Use This Workbook

Dive into sections based on your current needs—no strict sequence required. Each part includes:

- **Reflection Questions:** Explore your values, beliefs, and aspirations.
- **Practical Exercises:** Build skills and implement strategies.
- **Case Studies:** Gain insight from relatable examples.
- **Action Plans:** Turn your ideas into achievable steps.

Take your time; this workbook is a process, not a race.

Note to the Reader: To fully engage with the questions and prompts in this workbook, feel free to use additional paper or type out your answers as needed. This flexibility allows you to provide thorough, reflective, and meaningful responses.

Core Themes Explored

1. Authenticity

Discover how to remain true to yourself while navigating professional spaces. Define your values, build self-assurance, and balance authenticity with adaptability.

2. Resilience

Learn to overcome adversity with practical strategies, such as cultivating a growth mindset and turning failures into opportunities for growth.

3. Relationships and Community

Success is a collective effort. This workbook will help you:

- ☞ Build meaningful relationships with mentors, sponsors, and peers.
- ☞ Foster empathy and inclusivity in your interactions.
- ☞ Create a supportive community for growth and collaboration.

4. Lifelong Learning

Unlocking potential is a continuous process. Commit to growth through reflection, education, and learning from every experience.

Let's Begin!

This workbook is your companion on the journey to success. Reflect, grow, and take action as you unlock your limitless potential. So grab a pen, find a quiet space, and get started—your best self is waiting!

Chapter 1

Adaptability

Embrace Change and Thrive

The phrase 'change is constant' is widely accepted and endorsed by the majority of people worldwide. Others believe that in today's fast-changing and ever-evolving world, we need more than vision; we need to be able to adapt to change. This section will assist you in practical tasks to learn to build resilience, combat fear, and make change your ally.

Embracing Change and Adaptability

Reflection Exercise: Your Relationship with Change

Think about a recent change in your life. How did you feel, and what was your overall reaction:

_____

_____

What lessons can you take from that experience to effectively handle future changes:

_____

_____

_____

_____

Building Adaptability and Resilience

Growth Mindset Reflection

Think of a time when you successfully adapted to a challenge. What skills helped you succeed, and what lessons did you learn:

_____

_____

_____

_____

Practical Tools for Resilience:

Write three things that you're grateful for today:

a _____
b _____
c _____

List three small steps you can take to build resilience or manage stress:

a _____
b _____
c _____

Identify people in your support network you can turn to for encouragement:

a _____
b _____
c _____

Planning and Taking Action

What is one goal you want to achieve that requires adaptability:

_____

_____

_____

_____

List three skills or resources that will help you:

a _____

b _____

c _____

Outline a step you can take this week to move closer to that goal:

_____

_____

_____

_____

Risk-Reward Reflection

Write down one risk you are considering taking. What are the potential rewards and downsides, and how will you approach it step by step?

Example:

- ☞ Risk: Applying for a job outside my comfort zone.
- ☞ Reward: Career growth, new skills, higher salary.
- ☞ Downside: Rejection, feeling unprepared.
- ☞ Step: Revise my resume and apply to one role this week.

Your risk:

_____

_____

Rewards:

_____

_____

Downsides:

_____

_____

First step:

_____

_____

_____

_____

Affirmation Practice

Example:

- ☞ "I am adaptable and open to new opportunities."
- ☞ "I trust my ability to handle change."
- ☞ "Every challenge is an opportunity to grow."

Write three affirmations below to repeat daily:

a _____

b _____

c _____

Congratulations on completing this section!

Adaptability is a lifelong skill, and you're already on the path to mastering it. Remember, every step forward—no matter how small—is a win. Take a moment to reflect on your progress. Write down one thing you've learned about yourself through this workbook:

_____

_____

_____

_____

Celebrate this step forward, and keep practicing adaptability in your daily life. The best is yet to come!

Chapter 2

Appearance

Appearance: Presenting Your Best Self

Your appearance is more than just clothing; it's how you present yourself to the world. In this workbook, you'll explore navigating professional norms while staying true to your authentic self. Let's explore practical ways to enhance your professional image and project confidence.

First Impressions and Authenticity

Reflection Exercise: Your Professional Image

Take a moment to reflect on how you currently present yourself. How would you describe your professional style, and how confident do you feel in it:

___

___

___

___

What message does your appearance convey, and is it aligned with your goals:

___

___

___

___

Picture yourself in a professional setting where you feel confident and true to yourself. Write a few sentences describing your appearance and how it makes you feel:

___

___

___

___

Dressing and Grooming with Intention

What's one area in your dressing and grooming you would like to improve and how will you do it:

_____

_____

_____

_____

Confidence, Bias, and Action Planning

Building Confidence Through Accessories

Choose one accessory that makes you feel confident and consider how it elevates your outfit:

_____

_____

_____

_____

Reflection: Addressing Bias and Professional Norms

Have you experienced judgment based on your appearance? If so, how can you address or educate others about it:

_____
_____
_____
_____

Action Plan: Appearance Goals

What's one change you want to make to your professional look:

_____
_____
_____
_____

What resources or support do you need:

_____

_____

_____

_____

What is your timeline for achieving this goal:

_____

_____

_____

_____

Your appearance is a powerful tool for self-expression and professional success. By aligning your style with your values and workplace norms, you can project confidence and authenticity. Celebrate your progress, and remember—you're always growing and evolving.

Chapter 3

Authenticity

Embrace Your True Self

Authenticity is about embracing who you truly are—your values, experiences, and unique perspective—and bringing that to your personal and professional life. This workbook will guide you through exercises and reflections to help you uncover and express your authentic self while navigating the world's complexities.

Discovering and Living Your Authentic Self

Reflection: Who Are You?

Take a moment to reflect on your core values, strengths, and what makes you feel fulfilled. What are your core values and how do they shape your life:

Unlocking Potential | Workbook

_____
_____
_____
_____

Describe a moment when you felt truly authentic and how it shaped your

perspective:

_____
_____
_____
_____

How can you align your daily actions with your values more effectively:

_____
_____
_____
_____

Authenticity in Action

Overcoming Barriers and Building Connections

What challenges make it difficult to express your true self, and how can you overcome them?

Challenges:

_____

_____

_____

_____

Strategies:

_____

_____

_____

_____

List three people or communities that encourage your authenticity and how you can strengthen these connections:

a _____
b _____
c _____

What is one goal where you want to express more authenticity:

_____
_____
_____

Write three steps you can take today to live more authentically:

a _____
b _____
c _____

Insights, Tips & Strategies for Young Black People

What is one action you can take this week to lead authentically:

_____

_____

_____

_____

Write a short message of encouragement to yourself

"My authenticity is my strength. I will embrace my true self by:

_____

_____

_____

_____

Take a moment to celebrate your progress and commit to living authentically. The world needs the real you!

Chapter 4

Branding

Define and Showcase Your Unique Identity

Reflect and Define

Answer this to uncover your unique qualities:

What are your top three strengths or skills, your core values (e.g., integrity, creativity, leadership), and what motivates or distinguishes you professionally?

Strengths/Skills:

_____

_____

_____

_____

Core Values:

_____

_____

_____

Motivation/Uniqueness:

_____

_____

_____

Combine your responses into a short branding statement.

Example: "I am a creative marketing professional specializing in building campaigns that connect brands with diverse audiences."

_____

_____

_____

_____

Audit and Build Your Online Presence

Evaluate and enhance your professional digital footprint. What does your current online presence say about you:

_____

_____

_____

Ask yourself, is your LinkedIn photo professional? Are there posts or content that don't align with your desired brand? If so, update your LinkedIn headline to reflect your branding statement. What is your new headline:

_____

_____

_____

Communicate Your Brand

Craft a 30-second elevator pitch to introduce your brand.

Example: "Hi, I'm Alex, a data analyst passionate about turning complex data into actionable insights to drive growth."

_____

_____

_____

_____

Take it further by connecting intentionally:

Write out five professionals to connect with, reaching out to one weekly.

a _____

b _____

c _____

d _____

e _____

Evolve and Grow

Answer this to ensure your brand stays aligned with your goals. What skill do you want to develop in the next six months, what recent accomplishment highlights your expertise, and what feedback have you received to help you grow?

a. Skill to Develop:

_____

_____

_____

b. Recent Accomplishment:

_____

_____

_____

c. Feedback for Improvement:

_____

_____

_____

Plan your Evolution:

Identify one area for improvement (e.g., public speaking, technical skills).

_____

_____

_____

Outline three steps to achieve it:

a _____
b _____
c _____

Congratulations! **Go out there and let the world see your brilliance!**

Chapter 5

Career

Navigating Your Path to Success

Define Your Career Goals

Reflect on this to clarify your vision:

What is your dream job or career path, why does it appeal to you, and what skills or experiences do you have or need to achieve it?

Dream Job/Career Path: ─────────────

Why It Appeals to You: ─────────────

Skills/Experiences You Have: ─────────────

Skills/Experiences Needed: ─────────────

Activity: Create Your Career Vision Statement

Write a one-sentence summary of your aspirations.

Example: "I aim to become a compassionate leader in public health, creating programs that improve access to healthcare for underserved communities."

Your Vision Statement:

_____

_____

_____

_____

While Building Your Network, Reflect on Your Current Network:

Who in your network can support your career goals?

- ☞ Mentors: ———————————————
- ☞ Peers/Colleagues: ——————————
- ☞ Industry Contacts: ——————————

Activity: Expand Your Network

Identify three new people or groups to connect with and plan how to reach them.

a _____

b _____

c _____

What is your Action Plan towards connecting with them:

_____

_____

_____

_____

What opportunities can help you build skills and expertise?

Internships/Externships:

_____

_____

Insights, Tips & Strategies for Young Black People

Volunteer Work:

_____

_____

Part-Time/Freelance Work:

_____

_____

Activity: Plan Your Next Move

Write one specific step to gain more experience in the next month:

_____

_____

Preparing for Job Applications

Reflect on Key Application Elements. Mention three accomplishments:

_____

_____

Identify your strengths:

_____

_____

Draft a cover letter opening:

_____

_____

Activity: Practice Interview Questions

Prepare answers to these:

- ☞ Tell me about yourself.
- ☞ What is your greatest strength?
- ☞ Why do you want this job?

Reflect on Challenges:

What barriers might you face, and how can you overcome them?

Challenge:

_____

_____

Solution:

_____

_____

Activity: Build Resilience

Write an affirmation to remind yourself of your strengths.

Example: "I am capable and resourceful, and I can navigate any challenge that comes my way."

_____

_____

_____

_____

Creating Your Career Roadmap

Outline Your Goals Using the Table Below:

Goal	Timeline	First Step
Short-Term Goal #1		
Short-Term Goal #2		
Long-Term Goal #1		

Congratulations on completing this section! Your career journey is uniquely yours, and every step forward—no matter how small—is a step toward your dreams.

What's one thing you'll do this week to move closer to your goal?

_____

_____

_____

_____

Keep believing in yourself, and don't be afraid to seek help and opportunities. You've got this!

Chapter 6

Character

Building Integrity and Resilience

Character defines who you are when no one is watching. It's the foundation of your personal and professional life, shaping how you respond to challenges and treat others. This section on Character will guide you through practical exercises to reflect on, strengthen, and embody your character. Let's start building a legacy of integrity, resilience, and authenticity.

Understanding Your Values

Exercise: Discover Your Core Values

Take a moment to reflect on the principles that guide your decisions and actions.

What are the values that are most important to you, and why are these important to you and influence your decisions daily?

_____

_____

_____

_____

Cultivating Integrity

Activity: Reflect on Past Decisions

Think about a situation where you made a difficult decision based on your values. Describe the situation:

_____

_____

What challenges did you face in making the decision:

_____

_____

_____

How did staying true to your values impact the outcome:

_____

_____

_____

_____

Exercise: Integrity Check-In

Do you consistently follow through on commitments, act transparently in your actions and decisions, and how can you improve integrity in small, daily actions:

_____

_____

_____

_____

Building Resilience

Activity: Strengthening Your Inner Resolve

Think of a recent setback. How did you handle it and the lesson learnt?

_____

_____

_____

_____

Write one positive affirmation to remind yourself of your strength:

_____

_____

_____

_____

Exercise: Create Your Resilience Toolkit

Write out three strategies to help you cope with challenges:

_____

_____

_____

_____

Leading with Character

Activity: Character in Action

Identify a moment where your character can influence others positively. What situation can you lead by example:

_____

_____

_____

_____

What actions will you take to model integrity and resilience:

_____

_____

_____

_____

Exercise: Role Model Reflection

Think about someone you admire for their character. Who is this person, and what qualities do they embody:

_____

_____

How can you emulate these qualities in your life:

_____

_____

Your Character Growth Plan

Exercise: Set a Character Goal

Choose one area of your character to develop further. Which quality will you focus on (e.g., honesty, patience, empathy):

_____

_____

_____

_____

What specific actions will you take to grow in this area?

Action 1: _____

Action 2: _____

Action 3: _____

How will you measure your progress:

_____

_____

_____

Celebrate Your Growth

So, what's one thing you've learned about your character through this section:

_____

_____

_____

_____

Remember that character is a lifelong journey. Keep striving, reflecting, and growing. Your integrity and resilience have the power to inspire others.

Chapter 7

Communication

Mastering the Art of Connection

Strong communication skills empower you to thrive in diverse professional environments, whether through writing, speaking, or presenting. This section guides you through practical activities and self-reflection to sharpen your communication abilities.

Understanding Your Communication Style

Exercise: Reflect on Your Communication

Describe your communication style (e.g., formal, casual, empathetic, assertive):

_____

_____

_____

Name one communication strength:

_____
_____
_____
_____

What's one area you want to improve:

_____
_____
_____
_____

Enhancing Written Communication

Exercise: Analyze Your Writing

Look at a recent complicated communication you wrote. Look at it in comparison to the below checklist.

Checklist:

- ☞ Was it clear, concise and professional?
- ☞ Did it address the recipients concerns?
- ☞ Was it free of grammatical/spelling errors?

Could you improve it? If so, how:

_____
_____
_____
_____

Speaking with Confidence

Exercise: Craft Your Elevator Pitch

Example: "Hi, I'm Alex, a digital marketer specializing in impactful campaigns."

_____
_____
_____
_____

Ask yourself, was it clear and concise? Did it convey what you wanted your audience to know about you?

Activity: Public Speaking Practice

Choose a topic and present it for 2 minutes.

Reflection: What went well:

_____

_____

_____

_____

What could be improved:

_____

_____

_____

_____

Emotional Regulation in Communication

Exercise: Reflect on a Challenging Situation. Describe what happened:

_____

_____

_____

_____

How did emotions affect your message:

_____

_____

What would you do differently:

_____

_____

_____

_____

Code-Switching for Professional Success

Exercise: Identify Code-Switching Moments. How do you adjust tone/language with friends vs. colleagues?

_____

_____

Benefits of professional code-switching:

_____

_____

Activity: Practice Code-Switching

Write two versions of a topic:

Casual with a friend:

_____

_____

_____

Professional with a manager:

_____

_____

Wrap-Up: Your Communication Growth Plan

One skill to focus on this month:

_____

_____

Daily habit to practice it:

_____

_____

Feedback source:

_____

_____

Chapter 8

Diversity, Equity, and Inclusion (DEI)

Creating Inclusive Excellence

Self-Awareness and Valuing Diversity

Rate yourself on a scale of 1–5 (1 = Never, 5 = Often):

a. I reflect on how my cultural background influences my decisions. [——]

b. I try to learn about other cultures and their customs. [——]

c. I feel comfortable adapting my communication style to different cultural norms. [——]

What were your score(s)? Did they tell you anything about yourself?

Lowest score:

_____

_____

Steps to improve:

_____

_____

Activity: Perspective Shift

Imagine being a new hire where everyone speaks a different language than you.

How would you feel?

_____

_____

What challenges might you face?

_____

_____

What support would help you succeed?

_____

_____

Promoting Equity and Inclusion

Exercise: Advocating for Equity

Scenario: A colleague notices junior staff's input is often overlooked in meetings.

How would you address this concern:

_____

_____

Steps to ensure junior staff feel heard:

_____

_____

_____

_____

Wrap-Up:

One thing you learned from this chapter in the book:

_____

_____

_____

_____

How can you hold yourself accountable to advocating for diversity, equity and inclusion:

_____

_____

_____

_____

Diversity, equity, and inclusion are not destinations but continuous journeys. By committing to growth, understanding, and action, you're shaping a more inclusive and equitable world. Keep striving, learning, and leading!

Chapter 9

Education

Unlocking Opportunities Through Learning

Education is a powerful tool that shapes your career, enhances personal growth, and builds resilience. This workbook is designed to help you explore educational opportunities, plan your path, and confidently navigate challenges. Let's take actionable steps to achieve your goals through education!

Understanding Education and Its Value

Activity: Visualize Your Future

How does education contribute to your success in five years:

_____

_____

_____

_____

List three skills or knowledge areas you'll need to achieve your goals:

a _____

b _____

c _____

Exercise: Education's Career Impact

Write three ways education can enhance your professional growth:

a _____

b _____

c _____

Planning Your Educational Path

Activity: Research and Design

Choose one type of institution to explore (e.g., HBCU, trade school):

Institution type:

_____

_____

List three important factors in choosing an institution:

a _____

b _____

c _____

Research three institutions that match your preferences:

    a. Institution 1: ──────────────────

    b. Institution 2: ──────────────────

    c. Institution 3: ──────────────────

Exercise: Design Your Ideal Experience

Describe your dream educational experience, including courses, extracurricular activities and support systems:

_____

_____

_____

_____

Taking Action and Exploring Alternatives

Activity: Financial Aid Checklist

    a. Researched scholarships and grants.

    b. Completed FAFSA

    c. Explored state and local financial aid opportunities

Exercise: Scholarship Search

List three scholarships and one action you will take to apply for each:

a. Scholarship 1:

_____

_____

b. Scholarship 2:

_____

_____

c. Scholarship 3:

_____

_____

Chapter 10

Emotional Intelligence

Emotional Intelligence: Developing the Skills for Personal and Professional Success

Emotional Intelligence (EI) is a game-changer for your career and relationships. This section is constructed to help you reflect, practice, and enhance your EI in practical ways. Through interactive activities and self-assessments, you'll deepen your self-awareness, strengthen your social skills, and build empathy—essential for thriving in any environment.

Unlocking Potential | Workbook

Self-Awareness and Regulation

Interactive Exercise: KnowYourself

What situations commonly trigger strong emotions for you:

_____

_____

How do you usually respond when overwhelmed:

_____

_____

List three emotions you felt strongly this week and their causes:

a. Emotion 1:

_____

_____

_____

b. Emotion 2:

_____
_____
_____

c. Emotion 3:

_____
_____
_____

Activity: Mindfulness in Action

Spend 5 minutes practicing mindfulness. Focus on your breath and gently redirect wandering thoughts. How did mindfulness help you:

_____
_____
_____

Scenario Practice: Staying Composed

Scenario: A colleague unfairly criticizes your work in a meeting. What is your immediate reaction:

_____

_____

What is your plan to stay composed:

_____

_____

Emotional Regulation Toolkit

Choose a strategy to try this week. Be mindful of which technique(s) worked best for you:

- ☞ Deep breaths before responding
- ☞ Calming mantra (e.g., "Stay calm, stay focused")
- ☞ Writing feelings before reacting

Empathy and Social Skills

Exercise: Walking in Their Shoes

Choose someone you interact with regularly. What challenges might they face:

_____

_____

How can you show support:

_____

_____

Activity: Empathy Journal

For three days, record one empathetic interaction:

Who was involved?

_____

What did you do?

_____

_____

How did they respond?

_____

_____

Role Play: Difficult Conversations

Scenario: A teammate repeatedly misses deadlines. Draft a thoughtful and respectful response:

_____

_____

Building Stronger Connections

Choose one action this week:

- ☞ Ask a colleague about their weekend.
- ☞ Share feedback with kindness.
- ☞ Offer help to someone struggling.

Motivation and Growth

Exercise: Define Your Goals

Professional Goal: _____

Personal Goal: _____

What motivates you to achieve these goals:

_____

_____

_____

_____

Personal Commitment

Complete the sentence: I commit to improving my emotional intelligence by:

_____

_____

Reflection and Growth

What did you learn about yourself in this chapter:

_____

_____

_____

Unlocking Potential | Workbook

What skill are you excited to continue practicing:

_____

_____

_____

How will you measure progress:

_____

_____

Chapter 11

Entrepreneurship

Turning Vision Into Reality

Entrepreneurship is about more than starting a business; it's about shaping your future, chasing your passion, and creating meaningful impact. Let's guide you through the key stages of entrepreneurship, helping you develop your ideas, overcome challenges, and stay motivated. The journey will be transformative, so brace yourself!

Define Your Vision and Readiness

Activity: Define Your Why

Why do you want to become an entrepreneur:

_____

_____

Unlocking Potential | Workbook

What problem do you want to solve or value do you want to create:

_____

_____

_____

What is your vision:

_____

_____

_____

How will entrepreneurship impact your life and community:

_____

_____

_____

Interactive Exercise: Evaluate Your Readiness

Rate yourself 1–5 (1 = Not Ready, 5 = Fully Ready):

- ☞ Comfortable with taking risks: _____
- ☞ Willing to invest time and effort: _____
- ☞ Open to learning from failures: _____

Reflection: What's one area you'd like to improve?

Your answer: _____

Discover and Validate Your Business Idea

Exercise: Brainstorm Opportunities

What are your skills or passions:

_____

What problems or market gaps have you noticed:

Unlocking Potential | Workbook

Where do your passions and market needs intersect:

_____

_____

Activity: Validate Your Idea

Use this checklist:

- ☞ Does it solve a real problem
- ☞ Do you have a defined target customer(s)
- ☞ Do you have a monetizable idea (can you make money off of it)
- ☞ What is your competitive advantage

Next Step: What's one action to research your idea this week:

_____

_____

Build Your Plan and Take Action

Exercise: Map Out Your Business Plan

Business idea and the problem it solves:

_____

_____

Target customers:

_____

_____

Products/Services offered:

_____

_____

Marketing strategy:

_____

_____

Financial projections (costs, revenue, profit):

_____

_____

Activity: Funding Your Dream

Potential funding sources:

- Personal savings: ―――――――――――――
- Loans or Grants: ―――――――――――――
- Crowdfunding: ―――――――――――――

Next Step: What action will you take to secure funding?

Your step:

_____

_____

Wrap-Up: Your Action Plan

Immediate step toward your entrepreneurial goal:

_____

_____

_____

_____

Habit to stay motivated:

_____

_____

Accountability partner:

_____

_____

_____

Chapter 12

Finance

Building A Strong Financial Future

---◆◇◆---

Managing your finances can feel challenging and overwhelming, but this section simplifies the process. Let's explore how to make finances manageable, practical, and engaging!

Building Your Budget and Managing Finances

Activity: Map Your Finances

Write down your monthly income:

_____

_____

List your monthly expenses:

a. Needs (50%):

_____

_____

b. Wants (30%):

_____

_____

c. Savings/Debt (20%):

_____

_____

Exercise: Create Your Ideal Budget

Calculate based on the 50/30/20 rule:

a. Needs (50%): $ _____

b. Wants (30%): $ _____

c. Savings/Debt (20%): $ _____

Reflection: What adjustment will you make to align your budget?

_____

_____

_____

Saving and Managing Debt

Interactive Exercise: Set Financial Goals

- ☞ Short-term goal (1–3 months): ―――――
- ☞ Long-term goal (1–5 years): ―――――

Steps to achieve:

a _____

b _____

c _____

d _____

Activity: Start Saving

Weekly saving amount: $ ―――――――――

Savings method:

- ☞ High-yield account
- ☞ Automate paycheck savings
- ☞ Use a savings app

Building Financial Wellness

Exercise: Manage Financial Stress

Your biggest financial worry:

_____

_____

Steps to address it:

a _____

b _____

c _____

_____

Activity: Build Your Support System

Trusted financial advisor or mentor:

_____

_____

Financial app or tool:

_____

_____

Resource (book, website):

_____

_____

Final Action Plan

One action to improve your finances this month:

_____

_____

Insights, Tips & Strategies for Young Black People

Celebrate small wins (e.g., paying off a debt):

_____

_____

Your ultimate financial goal(s):

_____

_____

Chapter 13

Goal Setting

Your Path to Purposeful Success

Crafting SMART Goals

Activity: Define A SMART Goal

Specific: What do you want to achieve:

_____

_____

_____

Measurable: How will you track progress:

_____

_____

_____

Achievable: Why is this goal realistic:

_____

_____

Relevant: How does this align with your broader objectives:

_____

_____

Time-bound: When will you achieve it:

_____

_____

Action Planning and Accountability
Exercise: Break Down Your Goal

Step 1:

_____

_____

Step 2:

_____

_____

Step 3:

_____

_____

Activity: Accountability Partner

Partner's Name: _____

Support Plan:

_____

_____

Set Incremental Milestones

a. Short-term (week): _____
b. Medium-term (month): _____
c. Long-term (quarter): _____

Staying Motivated and Overcoming Obstacles

Reflection: Overcoming Challenges

Challenge:

_____

_____

Solution:

_____

_____

Challenge:

_____

_____

Solution:

_____

_____

Unlocking Potential | Workbook

Activity: Visualize Success

Describe or draw what achieving your goal looks and feels like:

_____

_____

_____

_____

Wrap-Up: Commit to Action

First step today: ─────────────────────

Habit to build: ──────────────────────

Supporter for accountability: ──────────────

Goal setting is not just about dreaming big—it's about taking consistent, purposeful action. You can achieve anything by setting SMART goals, creating a detailed action plan, and staying motivated through incremental progress. Keep this workbook as a resource and reminder that your goals are within reach.

You've got this!

Chapter 14

Health and Wellness

Building a Strong Foundation for Success

Remember, Health is the cornerstone of a successful and fulfilling life. With this workbook section, we will explore and enhance our physical and mental well-being while maintaining balance in all our lives.

Strengthening Physical and Mental Health

Activity 1: Your Health Snapshot

Current exercise routine:

_____

_____

Typical daily diet:

_____

_____

Sleep patterns (hours and quality):

_____

_____

Activity 2: SMART Health Goal

Set a goal using the SMART framework (Specific, Measurable, Achievable, Relevant, Time-bound):

Your goal:

_____

_____

_____

_____

Exercise: Stress Management Check-In

Identify your stressors:

_____

_____

Current coping strategies:

_____

_____

Mental Wellness Toolkit

Choose at least three strategies to implement:

- ☞ Mindfulness meditation
- ☞ Journaling
- ☞ Yoga or stretching
- ☞ Talking to a mentor or therapist
- ☞ Other: ————————————————

Achieving Work-Life Balance

Activity 1: Values and Priorities Inventory

Rank the following from 1 (most important) to 5 (least important):

a. ——— Career success

b. ——— Family and relationships

c. ——— Physical health

d. ——— Mental health

e. ——— Hobbies and relaxation

Activity 2: Time Audit

Track how you spend your time and identify areas to adjust.

Activity	Time Spent (hrs)	Adjustments Needed? (Yes/No)
Work/School		
Exercise		
Socializing/Family		
Relaxation/Hobbies		
Sleep		

Boundaries, Self-Care, and Reflection

Activity 1: Boundary-Setting Plan

Choose one area where you need better boundaries:

Area:

_____

_____

Boundary Plan:

_____

_____

Activity 2: Self-Care Action Plan

List three self-care activities for this week:

a _____

b _____

c _____

Reflect and Plan for Success

What is one small step you can take today toward better health and balance:

_____

_____

_____

_____

Remember, health is wealth, and investing in your well-being is one of your best decisions. Use this workbook to take actionable steps toward a healthier, more balanced, and fulfilling life. You've got this!

Stay committed, stay strong, and prioritize YOU.

Chapter 15

Management and Leadership

Building Excellence in Management and Leadership

By exploring core management and leadership concepts, practicing key strategies, and reflecting on your unique qualities, you'll become a confident, effective leader who inspires others. Let's get started!

Understanding Leadership and Management

Activity 1: Management vs. Leadership

Management: List three tasks focused on planning, organizing, or coordinating:

a _____

b _____

Unlocking Potential | Workbook

c _____

_____

Leadership: List three tasks focused on inspiring and motivating others:

a _____
b _____
c _____

Activity 2: Balancing Roles

Reflect on a situation where you had to manage and lead:

Describe the situation:

_____

_____

How did you balance the roles?

_____

_____

What could you improve next time?

_____

_____

Leadership Traits and Styles

Rate yourself (1–5, 5 being excellent):

a. ——— Vision and Goal Setting

b. ——— Integrity and Ethics

c. ——— Emotional Intelligence

d. ——— Communication Skills

e. ——— Empowerment and Delegation

Reflection:

Strongest traits:

_____

_____

Areas to improve:

_____

_____

Steps for improvement:

_____

_____

Activity 1: Identifying Your Leadership Style

Which leadership style resonates most with you (e.g., Soldier, Sergeant, Servant Leader)? Why:

_____

_____

Activity 2: Adapting Your Leadership Style

Reflect on a scenario where you adjusted your leadership style:

Describe the scenario:

_____

_____

Style used:

_____

_____

Outcome:

_____

_____

Building Effective Practices and Authenticity

Activity 1: Enhancing Leadership Practices

Task	Plan	Follow-Up
Delegate a task this week		

Active Listening: What strategies can improve your listening skills:

_____

_____

Constructive Feedback: Write feedback using the sandwich method:

_____

_____

Activity 2: Authentic Leadership Checklist

- ☞ Stay true to your values
- ☞ Embrace your unique perspective
- ☞ Seek supportive mentors and peers
- ☞ Continuously grow through learning and feedback

Reflection:

How can you align your leadership with Corporate Social Responsibility (CSR)?

Promote sustainability:

_____

_____

Foster community engagement:

_____

_____

Conclusion and Next Steps

What does being an effective leader mean to you:

_____

_____

One action to grow as a leader this week:

_____

_____

_____

Chapter 16

Mentors and Sponsors

A Sure Guide to Your Career Growth

Mentors and sponsors can transform your career trajectory by offering guidance, opening doors, and advocating for success. Understand the distinction between mentors and sponsors, identify the right individuals, and build strong, meaningful relationships!

Understanding Mentors and Sponsors

Activity: Define the Difference

A mentor helps by:

- ☞ Providing ————————————————
- ☞ Sharing ———————————— from experience
- ☞ Offering ———————————— to improve skills

A sponsor helps by:

- ☞ Advocating for your ―――――――――――
- ☞ Recommending you for ―――――――――――
- ☞ Using their ――――――――― to open doors

Reflection: Why are both mentors and sponsors important for career growth:

_____

_____

_____

_____

Finding Mentors and Building Relationships

Exercise: Identify Potential Mentors

Three qualities you admire in a mentor:

a _____

b _____

c _____

Who fits this description in your network (that is neither your mentor nor sponsor already):

_____

_____

Activity: Craft Your Approach to that person:

Introduction (Who are you?):

_____

_____

Why you're reaching out:

_____

_____

What do you hope to gain:

_____

_____

Tabular Activity: Expand Your Network

Area	Potential Mentor/Sponsor
Within your field	
Outside your field	
Across gender/race	

Strengthening Connections and Overcoming Challenges

Activity: Building Reciprocity

List ways to provide value to mentors/sponsors:

a _____

b _____

c _____

Reflection: Overcoming Challenges (How would you address the following?)

- A mentor is too busy.
- A sponsor doesn't understand your background
- You are Intimidated to approach someone senior

Reflection Question:

What three actions will you take this month to build stronger relationships?

a _____

b _____

c _____

Use the exercises above to identify, connect with, and nurture relationships with mentors and sponsors, setting the foundation for long-term success.

You're on the path to building an unstoppable support system—take the first step today!

Chapter 17

Military

A Journey of Discipline and Discovery

The military provides a distinct avenue for self-improvement, self-control, and leadership skills. Interact with the activities, think critically about what you feel, and take steps to determine whether this path suits your personal and career aspirations.

Exploring Military Service and Enlistment Options

Activity 1: Understanding the Basics

What, if anything, attracts / attracted you to military service:

_____

_____

Active Duty vs. Reserve Service

Activity 1: Comparing Options

Complete the chart to evaluate Active Duty vs. Reserve service:

Aspect	Active Duty	Reserve
Time Commitment		
Benefits		
Flexibility		
Career Impact		

Reflection: Which path aligns with your goals and why:

_____

_____

Leadership, Benefits, and Career Impact

What would be the most valuable military benefits (e.g., GI Bill, healthcare) that attracts you and why:

Unlocking Potential | Workbook

_____

_____

Activity 2: Career and Leadership Reflection

One leadership quality you already possess:

_____

_____

What skill(s) do you think you could develop through military service:

_____

_____

Name a skill gained from military service that could benefit your career:

_____

_____

Chapter 18

Networking

Building Professional Relationships for Success

Understanding Networking

Activity 1: Define Your Networking Goals

What do you want to achieve through networking (i.e., finding a mentor, exploring job opportunities):

_____

_____

List three industries or fields to explore:

a _____

b _____

c _____

Activity 2: Evaluate Your Current Network

Current Network	Gaps in Network

Activity 3: Practice Active Listening

Reflect on your listening skills during a recent conversation:

Did you focus on the speaker? **Yes / No**

Did you ask follow-up questions? **Yes / No**

How will you improve next time:

_____

_____

Building and Maintaining Relationships

Activity 1: Establish Boundaries

Personal and professional boundaries:

Work hours for communication:

_____

_____

What are topics that you avoid:

_____

_____

Draft a polite decline script for how you will deal with controversial topics you do not want to discuss at work.

Example: "I appreciate your enthusiasm for discussing [topic], but I prefer to keep work and personal life separate."

_____

_____

_____

Activity 2: Plan Your Follow-Ups

Draft a follow-up message:

Example: "Hello [Name], I admire your work in [specific field / achievement]. I seek guidance on [specific area] and would value your insights. Would you be open to a brief conversation?"

_____

_____

_____

_____

Follow-up schedule:

- **Week 1**: Reach out via email/LinkedIn.
- **Week 4**: Share a resource.
- **Month 3**: Send a friendly message or invite.

Expanding Your Network

Activity 1: Join and Engage in New Opportunities

Opportunity	Action Plan
Industry conferences	
Professional associations	
Community events	

Activity 2: Seek Out Mentors and Sponsors

List 3 potential mentors or sponsors:

a _____

b _____

c _____

Draft a message to reach out:

Example: "Hello [Name], I admire your work in [field]. I'd appreciate your guidance on [specific area]. Would you be open to a brief conversation?"

Reflection and Next Steps

Key takeaways from this chapter:

a _____
b _____
c _____

Steps to strengthen your network next month:

_____
_____
_____
_____

Networking is about authentic connections and proactive engagement. Build strong relationships and bring value to others for lasting success!

Chapter 19

Mindset

Developing a Successful Mindset

This section aims to help you develop an affirmative, growth-driven mentality that promotes your personal and business interests. Through various activities and practical reflection exercises, you will learn attitude principles and useful tools for attaining your goals.

Cultivating a Growth Mindset

Activity 1: Rewrite Limiting Beliefs

Identify one negative belief about yourself:

_____

_____

_____

Rewrite it as a positive affirmation:

_____

_____

List one specific action to reinforce this belief:

_____

_____

Growth vs. Fixed Mindset

Reflect on a recent challenge: Did you approach it with a growth or fixed mindset:

_____

_____

For an upcoming challenge, how can you approach it with a growth mindset:

_____

_____

Activity 3: Mindset Scenarios

Describe responses for each scenario:

a. Critical feedback on a project:

Fixed mindset:

_____

_____

Growth mindset:

_____

_____

b. Failure at a first attempt:

Fixed mindset:

_____

_____

Growth mindset:

_____

_____

Building a Successful Mindset

Activity 1: Positive Self-Talk

Rewrite three negative thoughts into affirmations:

Negative:

_____

_____

Affirmation:

_____

_____

Negative:

_____

_____

Affirmation:

_____

_____

Negative:

_____

_____

Affirmation:

_____

_____

Activity 2: Visualization and Vision Boarding

Visualize achieving a goal:

a. What does success look like?

_____

_____

Unlocking Potential | Workbook

b. How does it feel?

_____

_____

c. Steps to make it happen:

_____

_____

Create a vision board and place it where you see it daily. Reflect on its motivation. What were your thoughts:

_____

_____

_____

_____

Activity 3: Mindfulness Practice

a. Write about a mindful moment:

_____

_____

b. What did you notice?

_____

_____

c. How did it affect your mood?

_____

_____

Integrating Mindset with Goals

Activity 1: Self-Reflection and Growth Plan

Strengths:

_____

_____

Growth areas:

_____

_____

Actions to improve one area:

_____

_____

_____

_____

Goal Setting with a Growth Mindset

Set a SMART goal:

Specific:

_____

_____

Measurable:

_____

_____

Achievable:

_____

_____

Relevant:

_____

_____

Time-bound:

_____

_____

List 2-3 actions to achieve this goal:

a _____

b _____

c _____

Reflection and Commitment

What did you learn about yourself:

_____

_____

Write a personal commitment statement: **Example:** "I commit to practicing positivity and embracing challenges to achieve my goals."

_____

_____

_____

_____

Chapter 20
Professionalism

Professionalism for Accomplished Career Goals

Reflective activities, applicable tools, and productive strategies are incorporated to help you acquire some of the professional attributes needed to be successful.

Mastering Discipline and Time Management

Activity 1: Reflect and Act on Discipline

Describe a recent situation where you struggled with discipline:

_____
_____
_____

Unlocking Potential | Workbook

Identify one area to improve discipline:

_____

_____

Action Plan:

a. Step 1:

_____

_____

b. Step 2:

_____

_____

c. Step 3:

_____

_____

Activity 2: Overcoming Procrastination

Choose a task you've been procrastinating on and note what's holding you back:

_____

_____

_____

_____

Break the task into smaller steps with deadlines:

a _____

b _____

c _____

Activity 3: Time Management Audit

Priority	Category (Eisenhower Matrix)
	Urgent & Important / Important & Not Urgent

Unlocking Potential | Workbook

Elevating Organization and Dependability

Describe your current workspace and what needs improvement:

_____

_____

_____

List three actions to declutter and optimize:

a _____

b _____

c _____

Activity 2: Tools for Staying Organized

Choose a tool (e.g., calendar, planner) and describe how you'll use it daily:

Tool:

_____

_____

Integration Plan:

_____

_____

List the top three tasks for tomorrow:

a _____
b _____
c _____

Activity 3: Demonstrating Dependability

Reflect on a time you didn't follow through on a commitment and what you could have done differently:

_____

_____

_____

Unlocking Potential | Workbook

What is your plan how to ensure reliability in the future:

_____

_____

Professionalism in Action

Activity 1: Practicing Discretion

Describe a situation where maintaining confidentiality was crucial and how you handled it:

_____

_____

_____

_____

How will you maintain discretion in future scenarios:

_____

_____

_____

_____

Activity 3: Punctuality and Work Ethic

Reflect on a recent delay or missed deadline and its cause:

_____

_____

Set a punctuality goal for the next week and tracking plan.

Goal:

_____

_____

Tracking Plan:

_____

_____

Reflection and Commitment

What new habit(s) will you adopt to enhance professionalism?

Example: "I commit to embodying professionalism through discipline, organization, and respect for others' time.

_____

_____

_____

_____

Professionalism is not just a skill but also a mindset. Develop discipline, dependability, and organization habits, and build a solid foundation for your career. Use this workbook as a guide to practice and refine these qualities daily.

Chapter 21

Purpose & Passion

Discovering Purpose and Passion for Career Success

"Identify your passions, set meaningful career goals, and align your values with your professional pursuits."

This section is structured in three dynamic parts and includes engaging exercises and reflective activities to help you embark on a journey toward a purpose-driven career.

Uncovering Your Purpose and Passion

Activity 1: Self-Reflection

List three activities that excite you or make you lose track of time:

a _____

b _____

c _____

Identify three values most important to you:

a _____

b _____

c _____

Write one long-term goal that aligns with your interests and values:

_____

_____

Activity 2: Mapping Your Interests

Interest/Skill	Potential Career Path	Steps to Explore
Example: Love storytelling	Journalism, Content Writing	Attend a workshop, create a blog

Exploring Opportunities and Overcoming Obstacles

Activity 1: Research and Engagement

Identify one academic or extracurricular opportunity to explore:

a. **Opportunity:**

_____

_____

b. **Next Steps:**

_____

_____

Draft three questions to ask someone in a field of interest:

a _____

b _____

c _____

Activity 2: Overcoming Challenges

Describe a challenge you've faced while pursuing your passions:

a. **Challenge:**

_____

_____

_____

b. **Lesson Learned:**

_____

_____

_____

Strategies to stay motivated:

a _____

b _____

c _____

Aligning Passions and Career Decisions
Defining Non-Negotiables

List three non-negotiables in your career:

a _____

b _____

c _____

Describe how these non-negotiables influence your career decisions:

_____

_____

_____

_____

Passion in Action

Identify a passion to pursue outside of work:

a. Passion:

_____

_____

_____

b. Action Plan:

_____

_____

_____

Envision merging your passions into your career. Using SMART goals, how can you accomplish this merger:

_____

_____

_____

_____

_____

_____

Activity 3: Patience and Perspective

Reflect on a time you had to pivot your plans:

_____

_____

_____

_____

_____

Advice to stay patient and focused:

_____

_____

_____

_____

Final Reflection: Aligning Purpose with Action

Write a short commitment statement about pursuing a purpose-driven career.

Example: *"I commit to pursuing a career that aligns with my passion for helping others and my value of integrity. I will remain patient through challenges and focus on opportunities that allow me to grow while staying true to my non-negotiables."*

_____

_____

_____

_____

Use this material as a living document—revisit, revise, and refine it as your goals and passions evolve. Your purpose-driven career journey begins here!

Chapter 22

Relationships

Building and Maintaining Professional Relationships

Building Relationships

Activity 1: Relationship Audit

Fill in the table to assess your current network and identify growth opportunities:

Relationship Type	Current Connections	Potential Opportunities to Build
Mentors		
Sponsors		
Colleagues/Peers		
Industry Leaders/Experts		

Activity 2: Expanding Your Network

Identify three ways to meet new people professionally and add an actionable step:

Opportunity 1:

___

___

Action Step:

___

___

Opportunity 2:

___

___

Action Step:

___

___

Opportunity 3:

_____

_____

Action Step:

_____

_____

Draft an introduction message for networking.

Example: *"Hi, my name is [Name]. I work in [Industry/Field] and am passionate about [Interest]. I'd love to connect and learn more about your work in [Specific Field]."*

Nurturing and Strengthening Relationships

Activity 1: Communication Plan

List three people you'd like to strengthen connections with and create a follow-up plan:

Name	Method (Call, Email, etc.)	Follow-Up Plan

Identify two ways to add value to these relationships:

a _____

b _____

Activity 2: Intentional Messages

Exercise: Draft an email/ note to someone you admire.

Example: "Hi [Name], I admire your work in [Field/Project]. It has been inspiring to me, and I'd love to stay connected and learn more about your journey."

Engaging with Professional Organizations and Community

Activity 1: Joining a Professional Organization

Identify three organizations relevant to your field and outline next steps:

Organization Name	Why It's Valuable	Next Steps

Research one upcoming event:

a. **Event:**

_____

_____

b. **Date/Location:**

_____

_____

c. **Action Plan:**

_____

_____

Activity 2: Community Engagement

List one community service initiative to build relationships while giving back:

a. Initiative/Event:

_____

_____

b. Why It's Important:

_____

_____

c. How You'll Participate:

_____

_____

Final Reflection: The Power of Relationships

Reflect on one transformative relationship in your journey:

How it began:

_____

_____

_____

_____

What you've learned:

_____

_____

_____

_____

Revisit this workbook to nurture your network and achieve your aspirations!

Chapter 23

Technology

Embracing Technology for Professional Success

Building Your Professional Online Presence

Activity 1: Social Media Audit

Evaluate your current social media profiles and identify actions to align them with your professional image:

Platform	Current Status	Action Needed
LinkedIn		
Facebook		
Instagram		
Twitter/X		

Activity 2: Crafting a LinkedIn Profile

List three key skills to showcase:

a. Skill 1:

_____

_____

b. Skill 2:

_____

_____

c. Skill 3:

_____

_____

Using those three skills, write a professional LinkedIn headline that highlights your expertise:

_____

_____

Mastering Technology for Career Success

Activity 1: Skill Development Plan

Identify essential software/tools for your career and your action plan to improve:

Tool 1:

_____

_____

Action Plan:

_____

_____

Tool 2:

_____

_____

Action Plan:

_____

_____

Activity 2: Exploring AI in Your Career

Identify two ways AI could enhance your work.

Example: "Using AI for data trend analysis".

_____

_____

_____

_____

Reflect on one concern about AI and how to address it:

Concern:

_____

_____

Solution:

_____
_____

Networking and Professional Growth

Activity 1: Online Networking

Draft a LinkedIn connection message.

Example: "Hi [Name], I admire your work in [field/industry]. I'd love to connect and learn more about your journey. Your insights would be valuable as I explore opportunities in [specific area]."

Activity 2: Action Plan for Professional Growth

Outline three steps to enhance your professional use of technology:

a. Step 1:

_____
_____

Unlocking Potential | Workbook

b. Step 2:

_____

_____

c. Step 3:

_____

_____

Chapter 24

Volunteerism

Embracing Volunteerism for Personal Growth and Professional Success

Cultivating a Service Mindset

Activity 1: Define Your Values and Interests

What social issues or causes resonate deeply with you? **Example:** Education, environmental sustainability, racial justice:

_____

_____

_____

How do these cause/issues align with your personal or professional goals? *Example:* Volunteering in education helps develop public speaking skills.

Unlocking Potential | Workbook

_____

_____

Activity 2: Service Goals

Use the table to outline your service commitments:

Cause/Community	Volunteer Activity	Time Commitment	Impact You Hope to Make

Taking Action and Overcoming Challenges

Activity 1: Volunteer Starter Plan

Identify one local organization or initiative you'd like to support:

_____

_____

Draft a message to initiate a connection organization:

Example: "Hi [Name], I admire your work with [Organization]. I'd love to discuss ways to collaborate on [specific project]. Could we schedule a time to connect?"

_____

_____

_____

_____

Write a short statement to that organization about the impact you want to make.

Example: "I commit to [specific actions] to support [cause]. My goal is to create [specific impact]."

_____

_____

_____

_____

Activity 2: Advocacy and Impact

Brainstorm ways to contribute beyond direct volunteering:

- ☞ Write letters to representatives about a cause.
- ☞ Organize a community event.
- ☞ Use social media to spread awareness.

Reflection: What challenges have you faced or anticipate in volunteering, and how will you address them?

a. Challenge:

_____

_____

b. Solution:

_____

_____

Conclusion and Action Plan

How will you integrate volunteerism into your personal and professional growth?

_____

_____

_____

Future Steps:

- ☞ Research a new volunteer opportunity.
- ☞ Expand your network by engaging with professionals through volunteer events.
- ☞ Reflect regularly on your impact and adjust commitments as needed.

You can align your passions with meaningful impact by focusing on service and leveraging volunteerism. Let service guide your path to personal and professional success!

Conclusion

Well done on completing this workbook! You've worked through ideas, set goals, and explored ways to grow personally and professionally. This wasn't just about filling out pages—it's about creating a clear plan to help you succeed.

Remember, change takes time. Every small step you take gets you closer to your goals. Celebrate your progress, no matter how small, and learn from any challenges. Life is full of chances to learn and improve. The activities and thoughts you've written here are tools you can return to whenever you need a reminder of what you've achieved and where you're headed. Keep this workbook handy, update it as you grow, and let it show how far you've come.

You have so much potential, and your journey is unique. Trust yourself and believe in your ability to keep improving and reaching new heights. Whether you're building connections, learning new things, or working on your dreams, every effort counts. Now, it's time to put what you've learned into action. Use your talents, passions, and goals to make a difference in your life and the world. The future is yours to shape.

Stay confident, keep moving forward, and continue unlocking your best self.

www.ingramcontent.com/pod-product-compliance
Lightning Source LLC
Chambersburg PA
CBHW070629030426
42337CB00020B/3956